How to Evolve During the Trump Experience Whether Humanity Joins You or Not

Scott Grace

Copyright © 2018 Scott Grace
All Rights Reserved

No part of this book may be reproduced without written permission from the publisher or copyright holders, except for a reviewer who may quote brief passages in a review; nor may any part of this book be reproduced, stored in a retrieval system, or transmitted in any form or by any means electronic, mechanical, photo-copying, recording or other, without written permission from the publisher or copyright holders.

Robert D. Reed Publishers
P.O. Box 1992
Bandon, OR 97411
Phone: 541-347-9882; Fax: -9883
E-mail: 4bobreed@msn.com
Web site: www.rdrpublishers.com

Soft cover ISBN: 978-1-944297-39-8

eBook ISBN: 978-1-944297-38-1

Library of Congress Control Number: 2018960478

Cover Design, Editing, Interior Design and eBook Formatting: Cleone Reed

Author Photos by Jack Gescheidt.
www.jackphoto.com

A DEDICATION

I dedicate this book to my daughter,
Aysia Marie Grace,
and to all children
who will inherit this earth
long after Trump
is part of our past
and we will have moved on
to other learning experiences.

TABLE OF CONTENTS

A DEDICATION 3
PREFACE 9
   The Day after the Election 9
WHO IS THIS BOOK FOR? 11
DOES DONALD REPRESENT A DESCENT INTO DARKNESS? 13
MY HONEST OPINION 14
SPIRIT GUIDES 16
YOU ARE NEEDED NOW, MORE THAN EVER 19
THE JOY OF MAKING A DIFFERENCE 21
SEPTEMBER 11th— THE QUICKENING 23
THE TWELVE STEPS OF RECOVERING YOUR POWER DURING THE TRUMP EXPERIENCE 29
   Step 1) Admit that You Are Grieving and Do Your Grief Work 29
   Step 2) Whatever Qualities You Think Donald Lacks, Give More of Them 31
   Step 3) Preside over Your State—You Are the President of Your United States 32

Step 4) Hold Your Loved Ones Close and Express Your Love— Rinse, Lather, and Repeat Often 32

Step 5) Take a History Lesson...................33

Step 6) Admit that You Are Powerful 33

Step 7) Do Something Positive 33

Step 8) Deport Fear 34

Step 9) Take Up Drinking—Comedy that Is 35

Step 10) Welcome Major Changes 37

Step 11) Mind Your Own Business 39

Step 12) Connect from the Heart 39

THE TWELVE STEPS SUMMARY 42

DEVELOPING THE FEMININE SIDE 43

ATTITUDINAL OPTOMETRY— Reframing Things Till You Find the Fit that Brings You Peace and Joy..45

Reframe #1 49

Reframe #2 49

Reframe #3 49

Reframe #4 51

DON'T YOU JUST HATE THOSE WHO HATE?...52

And wouldn't it be nice not to? 52

SOME THINGS YOU CAN DO WHEN PEOPLE HATE 57
THE FOUR CHOICES 62
   1. Become Active! 63
   2. Become Politically Inactive! 63
   3. Bless Donald! 64
   4. Suffer! Blame! Feel Victimized! 65
ADVERSITY BRINGS OUT SUCH AMAZING THINGS 68
   Ah, the Media 69
   If It Is Helpful, See Donald as Part of a Global Colonic 71
WHY DESPAIR IS NOT AN OPTION 72
PLEASE DON'T POLARIZE 73
TRUMP AS A ZEN STICK 77
   Here are some questions that improve digestion. 78
   Free Group Therapy You Can't Avoid 79
BEYOND FIGHT OR FLIGHT 84
   The Third Choice 84
THE RHYMING APPENDIX 87
   The Story of Fear and Its Grand Departure from Your Nervous System 87
   Oh, the Places Your Ego Will Go! 92

Donald's Song 96
This Earth Is Our Earth 98
ABOUT THE AUTHOR 100

PREFACE

The Day after the Election

My daughter had been closing in on eight years old when Trump won, and I knew her disappointment.

She had been so looking forward to the first woman president.

I asked her if she wanted to talk about it. She did not. She wanted to go to the park and build a fairy house.

A fairy house?

Suddenly I felt angry at her for not digging into difficult feelings about a difficult subject.

Then I felt angry at myself.

Here I was, expecting my daughter to adhere to my standards of emotional honesty forged from decades of therapy.

And here she was, digging in the dirt at the park, beginning to build a fairy house.

I was not ready to let go of talking about the election.

I told her that I was feeling disappointed, frustrated, and, yes, scared. I asked her if she could stop for a moment and give me a hug. She did. She's a great hugger.

Then I started judging myself for sharing my fear with a child that was looking to me for her sense of safety, security, and grounding in the world.

From there I went on to worrying about how my excessive emotional honesty born out of too many expensive workshops might be passing on some kind of neuroses to her. Gosh, I can be overwhelming to adults sometimes, revealing too much information, especially on an emotional level.

Then I realized my worrying about the impact I was having on her was just another form of narcissism disguised as concern for her.

Finally, I laughed at the excesses of my ego, got down on my knees, and helped her build a fairy house.

WHO IS THIS BOOK FOR?

This book is for anyone who has been having trouble with Trump. It is for anyone feeling that your heart is aching and maybe even breaking over what's going on in the USA, and beyond. It is for anyone who cares not just about making America great again, but about the entire world, the air, the water, and all the children on the planet that are inheriting a future on earth.

There is wisdom here that will soothe and comfort you, and even parts that will lighten you up, bringing some humor where it is much needed.

Sometimes it will help you shed some tears that may have been waiting for permission to release. That's a good thing, don't you think?

It also helps dry your tears... and puts a smile on your face in the very next chapter.

It contains twelve new steps for recovering your joy and power through these challenging times while it feels as though the world seems to have gotten colder and crueler.

It is twelve steps that take you up the ladder of emotional well-being, not just for surviving, but thriving—that's right, thriving through this Trump experience, using it to grow and using it to flourish.

But, a gentle warning: This book does ask of you that you do some inner work. Those twelve steps are practical practices that you are asked not just to read and enjoy, but to, well, put into practice. The book holds your hand and guides you gently through that work. It helps you reframe what's going on out there in the world so that what's going on in your heart and mind isn't pain and powerlessness, but is actual hope and optimism, trust and faith, right in the midst of the chaos.

This book will give you a faith-lift.

It is scrumptious and healthy mental food that will help you more consciously choose your mood so your daily internal attitude is not shaped by a world so crude and rude.

DOES DONALD REPRESENT A DESCENT INTO DARKNESS?

At this point in our evolution, you might be wondering whether we human beings are evolving, devolving, or possibly both simultaneously.

My personal opinion is that we are evolving at warp speed.

For a rubber band to catapult forward, it has to be pulled back.

No breakthrough is possible without breakdown, whether it be the journey of the individual or the collective.

That is why twelve-step people end up being so grateful for hitting their bottom. It gets them started on their healing journey.

But whether the masses are getting off their asses or our species is too deep in feces, we might as well use the shift that's hitting the fan for our own personal fertilizer.

MY HONEST OPINION

I'm not fond of Donald Trump. He has no capacity for self-reflection, regret, and, therefore, growth. His arrogance is over the top.

He represents everything I believe makes America less than great.

Countries, like individuals, have shadow sides.

The United States has never truly apologized for slavery, Native American genocide, Japanese internment camps, and the Vietnam War, to name just a few of our trespasses. We have stuffed these things into our shadow.

America is like a sexual predator that has assaulted its way to "greatness," and has been in denial, refusing treatment or therapy, and continuing to think of itself as the greatest country on God's green earth.

Donald may be the best and fastest medicine for our country at this time to do some potent shadow work to heal that streak of narcissism, entitlement, and superiority that has impacted our relationship with the rest of the world.

You can't heal what you can't see. For the United States, our shadow is currently out in plain view. He is our president.

And the people who are behind Trump, wanting to *make America great again*, I feel their pain.

The middle class is vanishing, and people who worked hard to support their families and did the *right* thing, followed the *rules*, got a respectable job, are no longer able to support their families. Many have gone through a divorce, losing their homes, and see supporting Donald as a way to channel their rage at a system that has failed them. The plea to make America great again is an expression of grief, maybe misguided, but coming from a real sense of loss. The human tendency to cover grief with blame, to get tribal in times of personal pain and confusion, is understandable, and this book will help you have compassion for Trump supporters and not polarize against them, or be angry at them for polarizing against us. There is no real us and them, nobody to be against, just fellow human beings processing pain in different ways.

SPIRIT GUIDES

For some of you, the concept of having spirit guides might be new, strange, or impossible, according to your belief system. My experience is I have guides that I routinely consult for help, and they helped me write this book. (Yes, I have *Ghost Writers*!)

I believe we all have guides that help us constantly, and we can learn to converse and learn from them more consciously.

When Donald got elected, many of us—myself included—went straight to our egos for guidance, and thus straight to fear and revulsion.

Eventually, I had enough of the drama, and I meditated till I was still enough so I could soften and ask my guides for help. (This is a plug here for meditation, or anything that gets you quiet enough inside to hear guidance.)

They blew my mind by saying that they considered him the perfect president for this moment in time.

My ego asked, "WHAT???????????"

The guides offered me this metaphor from my own life.

When I started doing cleanses once a year twenty years ago, I used herbs that I now consider unnecessarily harsh, much too harsh for my body's present needs. But at that time my body was so clogged it needed dynamite to blast things open and get my systems circulating and balanced again.

My colon in particular was pretty full of crap.

Kind of like Washington D.C. has been for a very long time.

The herbs I used back then I would not use long term, but they did blast the dam and got the river flowing again.

Currently my ten-day annual detoxification uses herbs and practices that are much gentler. I don't need dynamite. I don't get headaches, diarrhea, or lose sleep like I did the first few cleanses.

Donald, according to my guides, is like my first cleanse. He is shaking everything (and everyone) up, and that is what is needed at this time.

They said gentler cleansing agents will soon follow, and they did not see him as president for long…four years ….or less.

They said we will look back at the part he played and be grateful. His ego may be in it for the limelight, but the bigger picture of our evolution uses him, ego and all, for a greater purpose.

Today's poop is tomorrow's fertilizer.

> *"It takes great learning*
> *to understand that all*
> *things, events, encounters,*
> *and circumstances*
> *are helpful."*
> *~ A Course in Miracles*

YOU ARE NEEDED NOW, MORE THAN EVER

Many people are quite discouraged (removed from their courage) by what is going down on the planet these days.

Despair currently exists in epidemic proportions. Many have lost vision for how they can help, as well as their hope for humanity, our future, and for the earth.

I have not.

I have something that gets me bouncing out of bed in the morning with enthusiasm. It's a safe and natural alternative to coffee, Prozac, and Viagra as well. It gets me up, inspired, pumped and ready for action.

It's not a pill, however. It's a point of view.

My point of perception is that I am a member of Love's Reconstruction Team, here on a mission to assume the position to penetrate the world with love without conditions.

By the way, feel free to substitute the word love with God, Source, Divine Mother, Higher Power, or whatever works for you.

I used to worry that my attitude was arrogant, and that I was suffering from delusions of grandeur. Now I understand that I actually am waking up from delusions of impotence.

Let's say it spicy: I am here to get it up each morning and penetrate the world with love, service, passion, and truth.

Donald has full unquestionable "confidence'" in himself. I believe many of us, myself included, can use more of that attitude, but in a balanced supply.

Unworthiness is just as much an ego trip as arrogance, and trips up so many of us from giving our gifts, from using our voices, and playing our parts in Love's Plan.

For most of us who are drawn to reading this book, our egos show up more as, *I'm not good enough*—than, *I am huge, the greatest.*

And we can learn to not take that unworthiness ego trip so seriously.

For more on this, see my poem,

Oh, the Places Your Ego Will Go

in **THE RHYMING APPENDIX.**

THE JOY OF MAKING A DIFFERENCE

In 1987 I lived in New Jersey by a well-traveled road. One winter day there was a huge storm, and the cars right outside my home were gridlocked for many hours, not moving an inch. This was before the days of cell phones and laptops, and people had plenty of time on their hands. I left the shelter of my house to observe the variety of responses to their situation.

Some spent the entire time grumbling their grievances, stressing the stress of their missed appointments, clutching their powerless steering wheels, never accepting, always at war with their predicament.

You could say they stayed in the denial and anger stages of grief.

Others made it to acceptance.

They got out of their cars to greet their new neighbors, making the best of things, laughing together at their shared helplessness. Children got out and played in the snow, blustery chaos a treasured playground.

A few people made it from acceptance to being of service.

They went from car to car to take orders for coffee and snacks. They braved the elements to walk an eighth of a mile up to the 7/11, and then graciously delivered the goods to their fellow stranded motorists. I noticed that the ones choosing to serve were enthusiastic and happy. The external temperature didn't bring down their internal thermometers. They radiated the warmth of their love, dispelling the frigidity around them with hot coffee and heartfelt generosity. (There, finally a sexual innuendo on the feminine side.)

So where are you in your grief process now that the world has been dealt the Trump card?

Denial, anger, bargaining, depression and acceptance are the stages traditionally taught and brought to the world by the authors and pioneers Elisabeth Kübler Ross and David Kessler.

I would add a sixth, which I would call being of service. Twelve-steppers know they have to offer help to maintain their sobriety. For many of us, finding ways to serve keep us feeling good and out of doom and gloom.

SEPTEMBER 11th—
THE QUICKENING

On September 11, 2001, I was glued to watching the news, like so many of us, feeling waves of shock, outrage, and fear.

Later in the afternoon I wrenched myself away from the small screen to tune into the bigger picture.

After some moments in the silence my guides began to whisper, and I took notes:

> *"This event is part of an evolutionary quickening, bringing about an increase of both darkness and light. Despite the tumult, the choice before everyone continues to be what it always is: To react with fear or respond with love. The media will mostly report and distort the reasons to fear, supplying the drugs for those with an adrenaline habit. You needn't go there, and don't curse those who still believe that an aggressive response will make them*

feel safe. Be of good courage. You came here for these times. Light your candle and find others who are illuminating the earth with love. Focus on the building of a new consciousness and a new world, even as this old one stumbles and falls like the towers. Stand tall and unwavering for personal and planetary healing, and you will live in the increasing warmth of your loving no matter how frigid the climate around you."

That was 9/11—the falling of the Twin Towers. Now we have Trump towering to grab our attention. He and his towers will fall too. All ego structures rise up, always to eventually turn to dust. Only love stands the test of time. Everything else… this too shall pass.

This is not summer vacation time on classroom earth. The curriculum is demanding, the lessons intense. The most fearful and aggressive people seem to have the most power. Certainly they have the most volume, being given a large megaphone by the media.

Is cheerfulness these days synonymous with denial? Are hope and optimism opiates for those with a lack of intelligence and an abundance of naivety? Will the meek really inherit the earth, and if so, how soon and where are they hiding?

Ringo Starr made a CD called *Choose Love*. Could he be on to something, or did our beloved Ringo do too many drugs in the last millennium?

Humanity is at a fork in the road. What will we choose as a species?

We've got some pretty big toys that can blow each other up in an afternoon. We've got climate change, and the means and intelligence to face that. But the will? The willingness to change? Many countries are well on their way to leaving no carbon footprint. But the USA and the collective narcissism that fuels our ego vehicles? We may take the longest to humble ourselves and change. Or be humbled.

It's easy to lose heart, or to close the heart to protect it from the rawness of fear, grief, and pain. But as Yoda said to Anakin in a Star Wars movie,

> *"The refusal to feel loss is a sure path to the dark side."*

Anakin did not face his grief and let his heart break open, and he soon became Darth Vader: His true Self was buried under a black mask and a suit of protection that guarded his grief and made him powerful on an ego level—but only temporarily.

Take heart, fellow Jedi's. If you are reading this, you are here to serve, and even your tears are a part of your contribution, as long as they do not come from believing you are powerless.

Did Martin Luther King feel powerless or discouraged because he did not see his dream made manifest in his lifetime?

I don't think so.

Planting the seeds and growing a dream is fulfillment enough, making for a thrilling and fulfilling life, as long as unrealistic expectations don't get in the way.

Humanity moves at its own snail's pace.

You and I, however, can move at lightning speed, as long as we mind our own business and not worry about humanity's pace.

Many of you have heard the story of a man who encounters a lady on the beach. She is picking up starfish one by one and throwing them back into the ocean after a storm had dumped millions of them onto the shore.

Her behavior is disturbing to him, as it holds up a mirror to his feelings of impotency. "Look around you! How can you feel what you're doing matters, saving just a few, in the face of such overwhelming tragedy?"

"It mattered to that one," she replies as she happily tosses another starfish into the sea.

To curse the darkness when you could be lighting a candle (or saving a starfish) is quite a waste of vital life energy.

To put it bluntly, it's time for an uprising—for us to get it up— for God, for LOVE... (I hear they are synonymous), and for each other.

In some ways the present may look like our darkest hour, but some of us can see and feel the dawn coming, something truly beautiful on the horizon— a new world being conceived and birthed. You are needed. You have a beautiful part that only you can play out.

So how, as this book title asks, do we use Donald Trump to evolve, whether friends, relatives, or the rest of humanity joins you or not?

How about we start with some soothing words to the parts of you that might still be in P.T.S.D. (Post Trump Stress Disorder), stumbling to find the serenity to accept the things we can't change, the courage to change the things we can, and the wisdom to know the difference?

How about a new twelve steps for a new sobriety while the world seems to be on a bender?

> *(Donald Trump just tweeted me that he thinks these new twelve steps are huge, the best steps ever!)*

So here they are: Please put them into practice. You'll be happier.

THE TWELVE STEPS OF RECOVERING YOUR POWER DURING THE TRUMP EXPERIENCE

Step 1) Admit that You Are Grieving and Do Your Grief Work

Grief work takes courage. It is not a mental process. It's not something you control. It can only happen when you surrender control. It's messy and painful and beautiful, and it is also a recurring cycle in everyone's life. Nobody escapes their seasons of grief. If you try to avoid it and push it down, it cycles and loops and repeats and drives you crazy and turns to all kinds of physical symptoms, anger, and depression.

But embrace and make room for it and it opens your heart wider than you ever thought possible. It is the doorway to both wisdom and compassion. What is grief work? It is pretty simple stuff. It involves crying, and that involves giving yourself permission and creating the safety to feel your sadness. As it comes. And as it goes. And comes again. This, too, shall pass.

Those who let themselves grieve well, love well. And laugh well.

You might need some help from a counselor or group if you have been used to living in your head and not honoring your feelings.

Uncried tears don't just disappear. They dry up into a dry, tough exterior and into a hardened intellect that is unwilling to admit fear or vulnerability.

> *Can you think of someone in the public eye right now who resembles that remark?*

Don't do *a Donald*. Don't get hardened. Soften into your pain.

Your quivering heart beats the drum of your sacred vulnerability.

Let yourself feel. It makes you human.

Grief is not anything that needs to be fixed.

It does need to be welcomed. Breathing deeply with a hand on your heart is a great way to get connected to your grief.

Then take some action that soothes you: a bubble bath, a hug from someone close, and/or a revealing talk with someone who can listen, support, and won't try to fix you.

Grief work awakens the feminine side, and we come from a culture that has worshipped the masculine and denied and judged the feminine side of who we are.

The feminine side is not just about feelings. It's about developing and using the right side of the brain, our intuition, creativity, and our ability to feel compassion and express our love. It is also the feminine side that allows us to tolerate and even celebrate diversity, differences in skin colors, different belief systems, etc.

Step 2) Whatever Qualities You Think Donald Lacks, Give More of Them

A) See him lacking kindness? Be extra kind to yourself and those around you.

B) See him as someone who always has to be right? Don't insist on being right about anything, especially how wrong you think he is. Look at your own attachment to being right, and have a laugh at yourself.

C) Do you see him as someone who is not able to respect people he disagrees with? Listen deeply to people with opposing opinions, and notice how they have the same needs as yours, just different strategies about how to go about getting their needs met.

Step 3) Preside over Your State—You Are the President of Your United States

You are the leader of your free world. You have both houses of congress behind every thought you think. You can cultivate peace in your inner nation. Donald Trump does not sit in your oval office. President You presides over your attitude, and the direction of your life.

Step 4) Hold Your Loved Ones Close and Express Your Love— Rinse, Lather, and Repeat Often

Tell them that it is in times of sadness and in the toughest of days where we often find our true mettle. ~ From a tweet by George Takei, the actor who played Sulu in *Star Trek*.

Step 5) Take a History Lesson

Our country has seen wars and grave injustices, slavery and even civil war in its past. Yet we found our way through. We will now, too. ~ Another Sulu tweet.

Step 6) Admit that You Are Powerful

Voting for Donald was an anguished 911 call for help from those feeling powerless. You are not one of them. Admit that you have power, a voice, and plenty of choices. You are a change agent.

Step 7) Do Something Positive

Do something. Anything. Anguish and anger without action eats away at you and is self-destructive. Add positive action, and anger helps to change the world for the better. Instead of focusing on what you don't want, channel the passion of your anger to focus on what you do want, and find some positive step to take. You might be inspired to political activism... or to set up a monthly recurring donation to Planned Parenthood. Is there an article inside you to write? Do something.

Anything. Rise up. Or get down on your knees and help a child who is inheriting our world build a fairy house.

Step 8) Deport Fear

Donald is afraid of Mexicans and Muslims, being criticized, and anyone who disagrees with him. He rejects others because he is so terrified of rejection. Don't be terrified of Donald Trump. Let the buck stop here. Only your ego can feel threatened, project blame, and build walls. Leave acting out the ego to Donald Trump. He's so good at it, so we don't have to be.

For many of us, Donald being President is bringing up our worst fears. But if it wasn't Donald, it would be something or someone else. Fear always finds something to attach itself to.

And fear is always
Forgetting **E**verything is **A**ll **R**ight.

Or **F**alse **E**vidence **A**ppearing **R**eal.

If you have forgotten that everything is all right, or at least everything is going to be all right, it just means you have temporarily tuned into some fake news. Change the channel. Build a border wall and send fear to the other side of it.

For potent and poetic fear busting, go to **THE RHYMING APPENDIX** and enjoy me as the Spiritual Dr. Seuss telling *The Story of Fear and Its Grand Departure from Your Nervous System.*

That poem will cleanse you of all fake news and get you feeling safe and happy again.

Step 9) Take Up Drinking—Comedy that Is

As long as Donald is president, you may want to drink in moderate amounts of *Saturday Night Live, Trevor Noah, Stephen Colbert, Jimmy Kimmel, Samantha Bee, James Corden, Seth Meyers, John Oliver*, and others who help us laugh at what is going on in the world. If, like me, you don't have a television, you can watch clips on *YouTube*.

But watch for the shadow side.

These comedians can also be quite polarizing and fear promoting, and I can't watch them too long before I begin to think that there are good and bad people.

And that's not helpful.

So I often take a break from even the comedic versions of the news, which, although can help release tension, can also support perceptions of how polarized we are as a nation.

I have joined the comic revolution by making up new lyrics to the song *Danny's Song*, by Loggins and Messina, as if Donald wrote it for himself. Instead of, "Even though we ain't got money, I'm, so in love with you honey," Donald sings:

> *"Even though I can't keep a honey, I'm so in love with my money, etc."*

For all the lyrics refer to
THE RHYMING APPENDIX.

Paramahansa Yogandanda suggested we see the earth as one big insane asylum in which we are all inmates. So laugh it up. Get those endorphins going. You can't laugh and be fearful at the same time.

> **Laughter is God's remedy for fear.**
>
> ~ **Alan Cohen**

Step 10) Welcome Major Changes

I studied with a spiritual teacher in the 1980's named Hilda Charlton. She had the gift of prophecy and saw things about the future that have been coming true before my eyes ever since. Over and over again she told us that as time went by, the light frequencies would increase on earth, and systems built on fear and greed could and would no longer operate in the shadows, and will be illuminated and exposed for the masses to learn and heal.

Think Catholic Church and sexual abuse going on for thousands of years and now coming out into the open for the healing process to begin.

She did warn us that the political and banking systems would be the last to change, as they were the most entrenched in the old energies.

She reminded us that whatever and whomever brought forth chaos was doing us a service, and from chaos would come rebirth and renewal.

Those of us who have faced major changes in our personal life—who have lost houses, security, incomes, mates, or have faced life-threatening illnesses—can look back and see how those calamities turned out to be blessings in disguise. They were like earthquakes that shook our foundations enough to get what was ready to die inside us to die, so we could do our grief work and get on with the creation of a new and better life.

Could Donald be playing a part in a global crisis that shakes us deeply enough, so that many who have been asleep at the wheel wake up and start driving in a positive direction? Or, better yet, get our egos in the passenger seat and surrender to our Higher Selves taking the wheel, equipped with Higher Power Steering?

In Chinese, the word *crisis* is made up of two words, *danger* and *opportunity*. These are indeed times of amazing opportunity.

Step 11) Mind Your Own Business

Byron Katie, one of my favorite spiritual teachers, is fond of saying that there are three kinds of business: your own, other people's, and God's. Staying in your business means minding your mind, guiding your thoughts and attitudes to a peaceful place and letting the world be exactly as it is. Or doing what you can about whatever troubles you and staying in the energy of building or being the solution rather than complaining about the problem.

I love reminding myself, when I get a little too lost in what is going on in the world, to mind my own business, to attend with what is going in *my* world.

Step 12) Connect from the Heart

I had a chance to put this into practice while taking my first break after starting this book.

The day after Donald won the election, I dived into writing this, as it helped me stay away from stewing in my own despair. But the beginning wasn't coming easy.

I needed help, so I went to the local java hut in the hopes that some caffeine and being around people would stimulate some creative juices.

An Hispanic woman asked me what I wanted.

An answer came out of me, completely unexpected, at a volume everyone in the store could hear.

"I want to tell you that I love you, you belong here, and that I will never let you or your family be deported."

"Thank you for saying that. I love you too. We are a community. We need each other."

We both fumbled around for what to do or say next.

I managed to remember that I came in for coffee.

But what I really came in for, what we all came in for, was to remember and demonstrate the power of love over fear.

We are here to take care of each other. Sorry if that sounds like socialism, but we are social animals.

And no president or political system can stop us from taking care of each other.

Ever.

In fact, the ones who try to build walls and make it harder for us to take care of each other are only serving to strengthen our resolve and get more of our feet moving in a positive direction.

THE TWELVE STEPS SUMMARY

Step 1) Admit that You Are Grieving and Do Your Grief Work

Step 2) Whatever Qualities You Think Donald Lacks, Give More of Them

Step 3) Preside over Your State—You Are the President of Your United States

Step 4) Hold Your Loved Ones Close and Express Your Love— Rinse, Lather, and Repeat Often

Step 5) Take a History Lesson

Step 6) Admit that You Are Powerful

Step 7) Do Something Positive

Step 8) Deport Fear

Step 9) Take Up Drinking—Comedy that Is

Step 10) Welcome Major Changes

Step 11) Mind Your Own Business

Step 12) Connect from the Heart

DEVELOPING THE FEMININE SIDE

I was inspired by a video I saw recently on *YouTube* from Matt Kahn, called *Anchoring the Divine Feminine.*

Matt is one of my favorite sources of spiritual inspiration these days. This video was made when Clinton and Trump were campaigning, debating, and offering *Saturday Night Live* some of the best content for comedy they ever had the pleasure of playing with.

Matt said, paraphrasing and doing my best to remember, "If Clinton wins, it will be business as usual, and things will evolve more slowly. If Trump wins, there will be much more shock and pain. But we will evolve much more rapidly. He represents the fast track."

He wasn't endorsing Trump. He just was sharing potentials he saw from his mountain-top view of our evolution.

His frame of reference is that we are witnessing in vivid color the collapse of third-dimensional consciousness, where polarities are always clashing and where having enemies, opposition, and threat is the norm. And it's all going to exhaust and burn itself out, giving way to the Divine Feminine rising from the ashes, according to Matt. And to Hilda as well, way back in the 1980's.

Meanwhile, those of us working on ourselves, cultivating inner peace, focusing more on nurturing than criticizing, are bringing about the awakening of the feminine—both inside of us and in the world. And this is the energy needed to bring balance.

Masculine energy, without the feminine as an equal partner, has brought the world to the brink of destruction. So we are going to need the feminine to rise up to bring balance.

I don't pretend to understand all that. Search for and watch the video if that kind of thing interests you.

ATTITUDINAL OPTOMETRY— Reframing Things Till You Find the Fit that Brings You Peace and Joy

In my coaching practice, I often serve as an attitudinal optometrist, offering reframes that allow for better (happier) vision, and helping my client adjust to the new fit. (Reframes don't always automatically feel comfortable.)

My favorite reframe, words that never fail to comfort me, came from the book, *Illusions*, by Richard Bach.

> *"The mark of your ignorance*
> *is the depth of your belief*
> *in injustice and tragedy.*
> *What the caterpillar calls*
> *the end of the world,*
> *the master calls a butterfly."*

The way I see it, the old patriarchal traditions are currently having their last hurrah. The good news is that racism and greed, misogamy and dishonesty cannot hide in the shadows as they have done for millenniums, and they are now being illuminated for the world to see. Homosexual abuses by the church, the Me Too movement—all the dirty laundry is coming up to be exposed and healed.

There are so many cameras around. It is time for darkness to come to light.

There is nothing off purpose about these times. It is awful, perhaps, at times, but not off. I prefer the reframe, awe-filled.

I was in awe listening and watching the young Florida Parkland shooting survivors speak from their hearts, truth to power, igniting a movement towards change.

I like to think of Trump as the perfect pawn for this moment in a larger chess game. He is, unwittingly and unconsciously, serving as the spark that ignites and lights forest fires in areas where there is a great decaying, and a great burning is needed.

He ignites passion and fury in people, a passion that I believe will get people to the polls in record numbers.

It was in the passion that Parkland survivors expressed so eloquently in their call to action, a demand for change. Those marches are just beginning. Let the youth lead the way.

These times are meant to shake us up, shaking and waking us out of our perceptual prisons, the habits we have of giving our power away by letting the outside world dictate our feelings and moods.

One thing I have found is that self-soothing is far more important than staying informed about what is happening *out there*.

I give myself permission to detach and disengage if taking in the news is giving me the blues.

But if you just can't pull yourself away, I hope you are taking in some of these reframes from your friendly neighborhood attitudinal optometrist.

This entire book is nothing but reframes, including the title. Yes, you can use this time with Trump to evolve whether others join you or not.

With reframes, it's never about the objective truth, but how we are seeing it that makes the difference. A reframe is a new way of seeing something, when you have outgrown your old frames. Here. Try on these new ones, these reframes. If they make you feel better, then practice keeping them on, adjusting your attitude to this change in your view of seeing, and let new, positive emotions flood your being—emotions like relief, hope, and optimism. Then you will be adding your upbeat energy to the world and not adding to the doom and gloom. What more can any of us do?

Reframing things starts as a mental process; and with repetition, it eventually brings about an emotional transformation, a change of heart.

And that is my job as an attitudinal optometrist. Offering reframes till something fits that helps you see and feel peace within instead of what you have been fixated on in the ongoing chaos of the ever-changing outside world.

Here are more reframes. Try them on and see if they help you perceive more light… you know you have allowed more light because you have lightened up about something that you previously felt heavy about. And if you have come this far with me in reading through this book, I know you are open to more lightening up.

Reframe #1

Political systems around the world have a job at this time, and they are doing it perfectly: Their job is to fail us, so that we stop looking outside ourselves and begin governing our lives and finding peace, truth, and power within. It's an inside job.

Reframe #2

Even if you see Trump as a detour—a huge mistake—detours and mistakes in the long run are often more valuable than a straight line to a destination. They certainly are juicier than a straight line. Hey, doesn't a straight line on a heart monitor mean death? So welcome the curves, the twists, and the turns. We are alive. Our hearts are pumping.

Reframe #3

Impeach fear. You can help impeach Trump, if that is where your passion lies. Not knowing if Pence would be better or worse, or if it really matters, I signed a few petitions that have been floating around. But as I understand it, that is trump change.

What will really change your life is if you impeach fear, vote worry out of your oval office, and bring more joy, community, and connection into your life. And you have the power in every moment to take steps in that direction, one reframe at a time.

And if enough people tend to their own happiness and evolution, there will be a tipping point; and the governments of the world will have no choice but to evolve with us, to reflect how far we as individuals have come.

That time may be a ways off, the enlightenment of our political systems, but your moment of personal awakening is here, now, in a theatre within you.

No more watching the trailers, wondering when the movie will come out. It's playing now.

No more happiness procrastination, putting off what brings you joy till your life is fixed and perfect.

It's fixed enough now. It's enough. You're enough. Give yourself permission to have joy. Give joy permission to have you.

Reframe #4

There is life beyond finding, fixating on, and fixing problems. There is so much wrong with the world, and so much right with it. The more you focus your grateful attention on what is working in your life, in nature, in the sky, and in the world, the more the things that aren't working take care of themselves.

I've been keeping a gratitude journal, writing down at least five things I am grateful for each night before I go to sleep.

I've also been meditating in the morning for a few minutes before any electronics or contact with others.

Feel free to join me. It feels good.

DON'T YOU JUST HATE THOSE WHO HATE?

And wouldn't it be nice not to?

Giving people the freedom to be stupid is one of the hardest steps to take on the spiritual path. Conveniently, opportunities to practice are all around us every day.

~ Thaddeus Golas, *The Lazy Man's Guide to Enlightenment*

Resist Not Evil

~ Jeshua Ben Joseph
(Jesus Christ)

When the violence in Charlottesville happened as the white supremacists marched, I asked for guidance about the rise in hate groups that seemed to come along with Trump's presidency and received the following:

> "Hatred and prejudice are just two of the many faces and flavors of fear. They have been part of the shadow of the United States since its inception. Native American genocide, slavery, and the Japanese internment camps all have been acts of hatred, born in fear, born from a belief that we are all separate and every man (or country) is on its own and therefore, our country (or an individual) has the right to get all it can at anybody's expense. The event in Charlottesville is part of a cleansing of the last remnants of those beliefs. Hatred is a mask that fear wears so it doesn't have to show itself. But the gig is up, fear. We see you. And in our witnessing we send you compassion."

Whatever it is that's bothering you on a personal or planetary level, imagine it's all being flushed out and illuminated. It can't hide from the light that is descending upon earth, quickening our evolution.

Like a pimple full of toxins coming to a head, there is a pop in the energy, and it all comes spilling out. Energy is moving towards exposure, healing, towards resolution.

It's all going to be OK. It already is OK.

The toxins that give rise to the pimple were in there all along, but the body of consciousness known as the USA (and other countries) can no longer contain this level of shadow in an unconscious way. So it surfaces on our complexion and pops. Ugly for a while? You betcha! Not forever, though. This, too, shall pass.

Love brings up anything unlike itself for the purpose of healing and release.

~ Sondra Ray

It brings me comfort and excitement to know that it is the increase of light that is making the darkness visible, and that it's all part of a healing and awakening for humanity. Narcissism, racism, and bullying cannot hide in the shadows anymore. It's being exposed and talked about on a regular basis, speeding up our learning process. More and more people, schools, and communities are standing up to bullying and even helping the bullies get support, as we can see that their acting out is a sign that they have been abused and are wrestling with some demons inside.

Trump tweets out his bullying like he has Tourette syndrome, an involuntary disorder. Perhaps for him it is involuntary. Certainly it is a personality disorder. But it is a part of Divine Order. All of it.

And as I mentioned before, another thing coming up for healing these days is the rampant disowning and disrespecting of feminine energy. The amount of men in power being called out on the way they have mistreated women is staggering. And it is all part of the entire world stumbling its way to elevating feminine energy to its rightful place: Leadership. Women need not just to be educated, respected, and safe, but it is women's turn to lead the way, women with awakened feminine energy.

It is the unhealed, unbalanced masculine energy that has gotten us where we are in terms of violence, greed, and wars.

Women who give birth and nurture life intuitively know how to lead with compassion. It is time for the rise of the feminine within us all. Me, too! That's the movement.

SOME THINGS YOU CAN DO WHEN PEOPLE HATE

First and foremost: Comfort yourself. Honor your feelings. Take care of your heart. Soothe your trembling, if you are trembling. If you are angry, find ways to express it, to move the energy. Pound and shout into pillows. Write letters. Call Congress people.

Next, if what I am about to suggest sounds repulsive to you, then more time and compassion for your pain is needed, but when you are in a place to do this…

Raise up your palms and send love to those who hate, to those who have so little connection to the feminine energy inside themselves that they feel threatened by diversity. Those who shout *America first* or proclaim white supremacy are scared stiff of the changes taking place so rapidly around them. Wish them peace and comfort. They fear their country and their way of life is slipping away from them. (And it is.)

Underneath the energy of the belief in any kind of supremacy or superiority is a raging sense of inferiority.

The world is becoming a melting pot no matter how strong the resistance and reactions to that process may be.

Racists and nationalists are not in control. The beliefs they held as sacred are in a dying process.

Their rallies, no matter how loudly expressed, are funerals.

Oh, how they would love to feel important by provoking fear and aggression in you, to get a reaction—any unpleasant reaction.

Fear, anger, hurt, recoil, shock, worry, disgust...

Don't react. Love them back.

Oh, by all means say no to their behavior if you are inspired in that direction. Vote. Speak. March. Put your money where your mouth is.

But don't polarize. Don't feed the "us versus them" mentality. See them as scared, rigid, sick, and suffering fellow human beings rather than bad people.

Let compassion for their fear be your predominant response. Jesus and Gandhi and many others will be with you in this endeavor.

Doing this may or may not impact them, but it will lift your spirits and open your heart. When you choose love, your own fear disappears.

So lift up your hands, send them love, and receive all the juicy benefits. Do it for yourself. Be a narcissist of the heart.

> ***St. Frances prayed,***
> ***"Lord, make me an instrument***
> ***of thy peace. Where there is***
> ***hatred, let me sow love."***

What courage it takes to practice and demonstrate that prayer.

So how might we do that now?

Wouldn't it be interesting to attend a white supremacy rally as peaceful people on the sidelines, not to protest or oppose them, but to just gently hold space, perhaps raising the palms of our hands and sending them love and witnessing presence?

Maybe we can even be playful about it.

I can imagine singing, "Someone's hating, my Lord, Kumbaya."

On the second thought, that might piss them off, which would not be fun or productive, but it is fun to fantasize about it.

So, in our imaginations, go ahead and join me right now in a round of Kumbaya. Imagine me picking up my guitar and all of us singing in five-part harmony, "Someone's hating, my Lord, Kumbaya," etc. Maybe verse two could be, "They could use a hug, my Lord, Kumbaya, etc."

The trick is not to react to reactivity with the same kind of energy back. Instead, respond with creativity. Bring levity to gravity.

And you can practice without going to rallies.

Raise up your palms now, tonight, anytime, and send out your love. Let Trump, his cabinet, his supporters, be embraced by unconditional, impersonal love. You can still disagree and oppose and be disgusted on an ego level, but ask to be a vessel where love heals all polarity.

Only love heals. And you will heal yourself as you do this.

> *"What the world needs now is love, sweet love."*

Burt Bacharach wrote the music, Hal David the lyric, and for God's sake, let's all of us feel it and bring it on, the love, sweet love.

> **"We can do no great things –**
> **only small things**
> **with great love."**
>
> ~ **Mother Teresa**

THE FOUR CHOICES

As far as I can tell, when Trump pisses you off or triggers your fear or sadness, you have four valid choices before you.

But before I spell them out, let's digress for a moment:

When Obama became President, many of us, including me, projected a savior upon him, giving him more power than he actually had. I held hope that this one person who shined so brightly might fix all the things about my country, and maybe the world, that I perceived to be broken.

I projected upon Barack my positive shadow.

Now, many of us, myself included, are projecting our negative shadow onto President Trump.

While Trump and his supporters might be projecting upon him the positive, a hero persona, I suspect that most people reading this are not.

If Trump triggers you, meaning that watching him, listening to him, reading or even thinking about him elicits fear, anger, or sorrow, please allow me, your server, to read to you four valid options from the menu, cooked up by my inner intuitive chef and attitudinal optometrist:

1. Become Active!

If you are activated, get active! Turn your anger, your outrage, into outrageous action... marching, organizing, and/or giving of your time or money. If you can't stand Trump, turn your attention quickly towards what you do stand for. Anger is only negative when it is accompanied by focusing on what you don't want. When you harness the passion that lurks within anger and direct it towards what you do want to create, you become a game changer. This is what fueled Martin Luther King. He had a dream and endless energy to work towards that dream.

2. Become Politically Inactive!

If you get triggered when you think of Trump, and you don't feel inspired to get involved socially or politically, then don't. And I mean really don't. Stay away. Do a media fast. Put your focus and energy where it wants to go.

Get out in nature. Don't watch or read the news unless you feel good about staying informed. Follow your bliss by consciously choosing ignorance. Give yourself 100% permission to ignore what is going on politically, and commit to filling your life with love and positive energy. Show yourself and your children that, whoever our leaders happen to be, we are 100% responsible for leading ourselves and creating fulfilling lives.

3. Bless Donald!

Whenever you do read or watch Trump, use the power of your intention to bless him. See him as suffering (he is) and doing his best (he really is). See him as doing good in the long run despite his Trump Towering ego. Send him love and light, and send love and blessings to the parts of you that dislike him intensely. The intensity of your dislike directly relates to how much he is acting out disowned parts of you. You may have intense self-hatred in your shadow about your own selfishness, and successfully keep it hidden far from your sight. But we all have it. As they say in the twelve steps, to see an ego is to be an ego. Or to put it another way, if you spot it you've got it.

So thank Donald for helping you see, integrate, and welcome home your disowned shadow.

The first three options involve a choice to do less complaining and more creating. It means not hanging out in conversations with relatives, friends, Facebook, or online chat rooms where the environment is filled with the smoke-filled conversation, *Ain't it Awful?*

Isn't it interesting that so many people who would never dream of polluting their bodies with tobacco, crack or meth will fill their minds each day with their mental equivalent?

This leads us to our fourth option…

4. Suffer! Blame! Feel Victimized!

It's a very popular choice, and so, on the bright side, you won't be alone. There are millions of people on this planet who will stand with you, blaming Trump, Congress, and Trump supporters for the mess we are in. Blame does alleviate the suffering a little bit, especially if you do it with some enthusiastic venting. So blame and vent to your heart's content! Grumble and gripe and enjoy your victimhood as best as you can, until you are bored with it, and are ready for something new. It's funny, but giving permission to consciously choose to suffer about all this lessens the suffering.

For me, I find that listening or watching Trump makes me cringe. And until that changes, until I can enjoy him as the character he is playing out without projecting upon him all my fears and unresolved issues, my choice these days is to avoid him.

Why?

Because I care about how I feel.

Do you? Do you care are about how you feel?

Have you made that a priority?

I care about what I put into my mind as much as what I put into my body.

I would not inhale from a crack pipe, so why would I inhale what the media offers me if it makes me smoking mad, scared, sad or frustrated?

Whoever is in the Oval Office becomes a projection screen for us to project what is unresolved in our psyches. Part of our maturation process involves becoming willing to stop seeing our president as either our savior or our enemy, and commit to leading ourselves, and maybe even our neighbors, and our planet, towards the world we are here to create.

I wrote a Spiritual Dr. Seuss poem you can find in **THE RHYMING APPENDIX** called *The Story of Fear and Its Grand Departure from Your Nervous System.* This may be a good time to pay it a visit.

ADVERSITY BRINGS OUT SUCH AMAZING THINGS

Although I was just a boy, I remember the 60's. I remember the excitement of the social and political revolution brought about by the need to stand up to Richard Nixon, military madness, and the hypocrisy of the Vietnam War.

The protest music, art, and culture that was born from those times still thrills me today.

And just a few months ago I changed the words of *This Land Is Your Land,* which is all about the United States, to *This Earth Is Our Earth.* Refer to **THE RHYMING APPENDIX** to read the stirring song I was inspired to write about taking our compassion to the global level.

Can you open your mind to the possibility that this remaining time with Trump can be, dare I say it, thrilling?

It's all about what you bring to the table.

It's all about where you choose to focus, your reframes, and what you do with your precious energy.

As always, there are but two choices. Lighting a candle in the ways you are inspired to, or cursing the darkness, being bitter. Love or fear.

Depression and despair are signs you are forgetting your power, curling up into a little ball of *ain't it awful,* listening to your ego's interpretations, drinking in the adrenaline and poison offered by mainstream media.

Ah, the Media

Have you noticed I don't have too many kind things to say about the news industry?

Let's face this sobering truth together:

The news industry is a for-profit business that is in the business of keeping you afraid. Fear sells newspapers.

If it bleeds it leads.

Fear grabs at your attention. Why does bad, scary news captivate you?

Maybe because you are in the habit of allowing yourself to be held captive.

By fear.

It's a habit shared by most people.

The news is addictive, processed, and packaged junk food for the mind, filled with tons of salt and sugar to chew on, swallow, and hook your senses.

Wake up. There is good news everywhere when you are tuned in to W-LOVE and value feeling good.

Donald calls all the news he doesn't like fake. Now that's not what I am suggesting. But if the news you are watching is increasing your fear and depression, turn it off. Not because it is fake, but because you are taking good care of yourself emotionally.

If It Is Helpful, See Donald as Part of a Global Colonic

He is serving the greater plan by bringing up today's shit, which will serve as tomorrow's fertilizer.

Join me in seeing Trump and his staff of toxic, abrasive herbs as a shit-storm colonic with a higher purpose in the scheme of things.

Vast numbers of people are getting fired up and involved in our political process like never before. Our immune system of citizens using their votes and voices was mostly dormant, hibernating. Now we have been rudely awakened. Watch out. Here comes change.

WHY DESPAIR IS NOT AN OPTION

What if America has had cancer for quite some time?

What if Washington in particular has been clogged and riddled with malignant corruption, gridlocked and unable to move forward and get up to speed with humanity's evolution?

What if Donald is like aggressive chemotherapy and radiation? From the poisons he injects, there might be quite a fallout, and not just our hair.

But then there will be a time to build things up, a time for healing.

While we are being interjected with *Toxic Trump Treatment,* we are going to need to support our immune system, and especially build it back up when the radioactive orange man has exited the body politic.

> *You and I are cells in humanity's immune system.*

That is why despair is not an option. You are part of the solution.

PLEASE DON'T POLARIZE

I was raised to be a true-blue bleeding-heart liberal/progressive, a smart, on-the-ball kind of person who would be disgusted by Donald Trump and all the people who voted for him.

That's my upbringing. But now I find it holds me back. It's not the current version of who I am. I love my intellect, but I don't treasure it over my heart, and I don't value it over my ability to connect with people I might not agree with.

The other day I sat on a plane next to a husband and wife who had been married for 52 years, and I made a nice connection with them. We talked a lot about our children. With joy and delight, we played *show and tell* with pictures on our phones of our offspring—my daughter, their five kids, and their numerous grandkids as well.

It was a long flight, and we three were in chat mode for much of it. We covered our hobbies, passions, and the music we love. I recited to them one of my Spiritual Dr. Seuss poems, which cracked them up. Early in the flight, I had a sneaking suspicion about them, and asked them a sensitive and scary question, as gently as possible. They validated my intuition by telling me that yes, they were Trump supporters. I had four more hours of flying sitting next to them, and I wanted to enjoy every moment, so I asked them questions about what they liked about Trump, what they hoped he would do. That helped them feel safe and respected, and it helped increase my understanding of what was in their hearts and minds. I felt no need to make them wrong, or even to express my politics.

> *"To accuse is to not understand."*
>
> *~ A Course in Miracles*

As we were saying goodbye, I gave them one of my DVD's of me doing my thing as the Spiritual Dr. Seuss. They seemed very excited to watch and share it with friends and family. We left that cross-country plane ride as friends. That felt good!

> ***Gandhi was once asked***
> ***if he was a Hindu.***
> ***"Yes I am," he proclaimed.***
> ***"I am also a Muslim, Christian,***
> ***a Buddhist, and a Jew."***

And so maybe I can think of myself as from a red, white, and blue state?

Furthermore, perhaps I can count myself a white, black, brown, Hispanic, Muslim, middle class, first class, coach class, lacking class, feminist, gay, straight, redneck, and transgender person?

What if we cared nothing about these labels, and took none of them seriously?

There would be no enemies and no need to polarize.

The unity that bridges our diversity is first and foremost of value to me.

Could it be that we are on the brink of a global crisis/opportunity, one that is so pressing that it compels us to build bridges of connection in response to it?

In the movie *Arrival*, visitors from outer space challenged the competing nations of the earth to rise above our differences and work together to save the planet. They created a crisis in the form of a puzzle that could only be solved by cooperating nations sharing information. Competition, working alone to fix the problem for one country, would have meant the end of our species.

Could our nation's biggest narcissist end up being a servant to humanity in spite of himself, an *Agent Orange for Good?*

TRUMP AS A ZEN STICK

"Nothing Real
Can Be Threatened."

~ A Course in Miracles

Donald Trump elicits a sense of threat in more than half the country. Yet, for many folks he is a soothing presence, like the way many people feel safer with a trained-to-attack pit bull in their home.

One of the first times I recall feeling a sense of threat was when I was in the first grade. We used to have what were called surprise shelter drills.

An alarm would go off in the middle of the school day and we had to march out of our classroom into the hallway and crouch down on the floor hugging our heads between our knees.

This was supposedly the safest position to be in, just in case a nuclear bomb hit our city.

One day I read up on nuclear bombs and learned how they vaporize human beings instantly, no matter what yoga posture one is in, whatever classroom or hallway.

From that point on, mushroom-cloud nightmares plagued my night life as a growing boy.

What they were not telling us was whacked!

Teachers of Zen used to whack students on the head with a stick when they got distracted, as if to say, "Wake up! Pay attention! Be here now!"

Here and now we appear to have a Zen stick occupying the oval office, whacking humanity with his every tweet.

Welcome to planet earth, currently populated with humans dealing with the latest installment of PTSD.

Having trouble digesting it all?

Here are some questions that improve digestion.

- Could Donald be acting as a colonic, helping to get the crap moving that's been hidden from public view and stuck in our system?

- Could this **P**resident **T**rump **S**tress **D**isorder somehow be a part of a larger and perfect Divine Order?

- What would Jesus do if he were around?

- Might he be advising us to love our enemas/ enemies, or might he advise us to kick the money changers out of the temple (out of congress, etc.)?

- Or some of both?

Boundaries and love can go well together.

Free Group Therapy You Can't Avoid

I like to see our collective adversity as group therapy we somewhere, somehow, signed up for.

Enter Donald, the generous provider of enormous (huge) opportunities to bring up Daddy issues and lessons in discernment for all of us. Daddy issues: Like if your father used his size and his power to scare you, to bully or manipulate you.

For many, Trump is that bully. And when we find the courage to speak up to a bully, we heal. Speaking up and standing up to an abusive father/dictator archetype helps us heal and complete generations of trauma.

For his base he's a hero with the balls to say and do the hard stuff, the courage to rock the boat. Finally, someone has come along who will stand up for our country and protect us from threats.

It's like there are two worlds.

In one, Trump is grabbing our collective pussy, violating our sacred feminine energy.

And in a whole different world, right here in the same country, Trump supporters are soothed now that tough Donald has our back, doing something about the invaders/illegals marching past our leaky borders/boundaries, taking our jobs, and terrorizing our nation.

Here comes Daddy Trump, towering to the rescue! We finally have a pit bull to guard our house, one who fiercely puts America first.

Those who feel threatened by him and those who feel he has come to remove threats are currently camped out in two diametrically polarized worlds.

Can the two worlds co-exist? Is there a national healing available when a sense of threat is so active in both camps?

Or perhaps like oil and water, there is some parting here that is unavoidable, a result of powerful forces of nature that can't be stopped?

Nature sometimes burns forests down to make way for new life. Trying to run around putting out fires is not always in our best interests.

Sometimes we have to let these times burn. Feel the burn. Learn from the burn.

And return, again and again, to some sort of practice or ritual, to that place in you that knows no threats, your practice of being at peace. This, too, shall pass.

After the fire destroys the old and decaying, new life rises from the ashes.

> ***A Course in Miracles* starts by saying, "Nothing real can be threatened."**

But then what do we do with our sense of threat that our ego believes is real and valid?

How do you heal, personally, when your nervous system is so freakin' nervous?

Perhaps it is so nervous because you've been trained to look outside yourself your whole life for your sense of safety, peace, and security.

For me, mindfulness meditation, *A Course in Miracles,* EFT tapping, inner-child work, and regular weekly coaching/therapy are all helpful in transforming the fight or flight energy out of my nervous system.

Deep breathing releases fear and helps me return to feeling safe.

But I'm also a big believer in the power of saying NO!

And in some cases, NO WAY! NO WAY AT ALL!

If, when you were a child, your sense of safety/innocence got lost or buried, then this Trump Presidency is your therapy.

It's your chance to speak up, claim your power, and heal the energy of past violation by standing up to present abuse.

If you feel inspired to shout NO at a perceived injustice or violation, shout it out with all your heart and all your resources, all your passion and creativity.

No slumping shoulders or head hanging low.

Now is the time to rise up. Not against anything. But *for* something.

BEYOND FIGHT OR FLIGHT

The Third Choice

The adrenal glands offer us two choices: fight or flight.

Then there is the pineal gland, the third eye, which rests in the center of your head and secretes fluids that help you realize how safe and how loved you are. It also helps you get in touch with that still small voice that guides your life and steers you to peace.

You know that still small voice? In tone and message it is almost the exact opposite of the loud, shrill voice that Trump uses. The more you practice valuing being at peace instead of being right, the more you can tune in and hear it, and ultimately give your still, small voice the steering wheel instead of being driven by your ego.

So what voice is more compelling to you: a still, small voice that's inside you, guiding you to peace 24/7, or the loudmouth on TV, stirring up the pot, creating drama, but only if you let him be a major actor on your stage. *A Course in*

Miracles reminds us that the Holy Spirit (that still, small voice inside you) is as loud as your willingness to listen. So work on your willingness and your still small voice gets louder, easier to hear, fully present in your mind.

Meditation and prayer are amongst many activities that open up the pineal gland. And when the pineal is open, peace is with you in a way that nothing in this world can threaten.

People like Jesus, Martin Luther King Jr., and Gandhi have shown humanity a way of resisting that is free of resistance, a way of marching for something instead of against, and rising up in an uprising that rests the weary adrenals and activates the pineal, which secretes the wisdom and guidance that triumphs over fight, flight, fright, and might.

We can then make the leap from polarized us-and-them thinking to a knowing that amongst the greatest diversity humanity has ever seen, there is still only one of us here, and only a win-win way of thinking will prevail. When you say no to polarized us-versus-them thinking, with your very presence you become a peacemaker.

Right here within this Trump experience there is a massive opportunity for masses of people to stand up and reclaim Lady Liberty, the welcoming feminine energy of inclusiveness that greets refugees and immigrants and says, "Welcome. You have opportunities here. And you have gifts to share with us. We are all in this together."

Trump and his outdated belief system has bitch-slapped the rising feminine energy on this planet. And she is not taking this lying down.

Her time has come, and she (we) will restore her rightful place.

Hell, we stood up to a tyrant king once before and it worked out pretty well.

These are exciting times to be alive, to own your power, and to know that you make a difference.

Chaos is such a potent activator of creativity, passion, and energy.

What will you do with yours?

> *"You are not a realist unless you believe in miracles"*
>
> **~ Anwar Sadat**

THE RHYMING APPENDIX

The Story of Fear and Its Grand Departure from Your Nervous System

Gather my friends 'cause the end times are near.
Not the end of the world but the end of your fear,
So turn off the lights; make it dark now, I dare ya!
Stick around for a while and I'm gonna unscare ya!

Now when you were young and most things were quite swell,
Fear knocked on your door with a product to sell.
And like most good *salesman*, he cast quite a spell
While selling insurance called *All Is Not Well*.

Now *All Is Not Well* came in its own case,
The case that there's danger all over the place.
And after you bought it, your *All Is Not Well*,
You felt it your duty to share and to tell.

And so mouth to mouth was how fear procreated
With no YouTube or Facebook to disseminate it.
Fear soon went viral all over the globe
Using old-time religion to dispense and promote,

'Cause fear knew the way to get globally big
Was to drive a false wedge between God and his kids.

And that's how he came to be so domineering
By replacing God loving with *You must be God fearing!*

Then fear and religion began co-creating
And cooked up a symbol of fear they called Satan.
As if infinite love had a worthy opponent
With pitchfork in hand who could strike any moment.

The concept was great for maintaining control
Making people behave as if they're on parole,
'Cause when God-fearing people are scared for their souls,
They put much more silver and gold in the bowls.

So business was booming and fear kept on spreading,
And fear loved the credit the devil was getting,
'Cause fear much prefers to stay hidden from view
And play hide and seek in its host, which is you.

"I'm not afraid, I'm just angry!" it shouts!
"I've been mistreated and need to speak out!"
"I'm not afraid, I'm upset, and I'm caring."
There's so many disguises that fear enjoys wearing.

He's proud of his wardrobe because he designed it
Though he wouldn't admit it, fear's quite clothes-minded.

So he doesn't realize that he's often dressed funny
Wearing layers of worry, looking like a stress
bunny.

And when you're not looking, he dresses you too
In stress bunny outfits that don't become you.
'Cause when you wear worry it wears tight and stiff
From statically clinging to imagined what-ifs.

Worst case scenarios fill your projector.
Then fear says, "Don't worry, I'll be your protector!"
He shows you his life insurance policy
And says "Here's what you get when you sign up
with me.

"You get top-notch around-the-clock security,
An armored alarm system on your body,
And if you're harassed I'm your personal bouncer,
And for making decisions, I'll be your guidance
counselor.

"No more will I let you take risks that could hurt you.
Just stick with me kid, I will never desert you.
Now all of your loved ones have already signed.
Don't be a black sheep; join the flock, you'll be
fine!"

So you signed up and breathed a big sigh of relief
'Cause you thought you'd feel safer with fear as
your chief,
But the contract had fine print too fine to be seen
And you didn't read the clause that denied you your
dreams.

From then on heart's desires that came to be birthed
Were blocked by your fears before they could reach earth.
It seemed your new policy's whole-life protection
Was more birth controlling than most contraception.

How could you conceive of a life more abundant
With fear in your ear like a Cable News pundit
Who's yelling, "I'm telling the truth, fair and balanced!"
While drowning out most of your love, gifts, and talents.

Now fear says, "GET REAL!" That's his bottom line thing,
And fear learned what's real from his friend Stephen King
Whose collection of books make outstanding addictions
As long as you realize you are reading fiction,
Which is what you can do with your own fear collection.
Just transfer them all to your mind's fiction section

'Cause no matter how gripping a tale fear can tell
Its original premise that all is not well
Is a bit topsy-turvy in this universe
And deserves to be laughed off the face of the earth.

And while you are laughing you let in the light
Which makes fear pack his bags and get on the

next flight,
'Cause he needs to feel needed and if you choose joy
Well, then fear has no choice but to be unemployed.

Fear used to feel needed when lions were chasing you
Gathering speed with intentions of tasting you,
But nowadays most of the lions we find
Are fictional cats roaming around in our minds.

And when you stop feeding the cats in your head
They just go away 'cause they're not getting fed.
And with a clear head you are free now to choose
A channel that's broadcasting much better news.

So you get off the couch and turn off the TV
And tune into W.L.O.V.E.
It's free of commercials with nothing to sell,
Just a steady reminder that all is quite well.

And all is quite well is insurance enough.
You're already covered by a plan you can trust.
You've got Universal, the original Plan,
And there's never a moment that you're not in good hands.
You're no longer buying fear's insurance scam
'Cause you know every moment you are in good hands

Oh, the Places Your Ego Will Go!

Your ego will travel with you on this earth
And be your companion for worser or worse.
It pretends it's your friend, your bestest amigo,
And it pours on the guilt; that's the mark of the ego.

It's there to protect you, to help you be strong,
So it has to remind you you've done it all wrong.
You're lazy, you're weak, and you don't have a clue
That's your ego at work trying to motivate you!

The ego wants you to be all you can be
So it gives you these pep talks all day and for free.
Oh, the places you'll go and the guilt trips you'll travel
As the ego plays judge and bangs down on its gavel.

But you always can get some relief from your shame
By projecting it on to the others you'll blame,
For that is the ego at its beastiest best.
It nurses its grievances close to its chest.

Republicans, liberals, your parents, your ex—.
The world is just teeming with folks to correct
If only these fools would conform to your ways
You could get on with life without further delays.

The ego keeps finding new gripes to complain about.
Turns molehills to mountains of yikes to feel pain about.
Sometimes the ego's stuff makes you so stuffy

You come down with a cold or an ouchy more roughy.

But there's no time for rest so get up out of bed!
If you're just here now and then, you won't get ahead.
Your to-do list must buzz like the bees when they're busying
Keep filling your days till they're endlessly dizzying.

Oh, the places you'll go and the people you'll see
All through the lens of *What's in it for me?*
For the ego believes there is something it lacks,
And till it is found it won't let you relax.

Perhaps you will find it in the next one you date
True love at first sight with a soul kind of mate.
The romance is hot till the climate turns cold
'Cause when two halves combine they do not make a whole.
It's fine till the love gets obscured by control
'Cause when two halves collide they cannot make a whole.

So the ego moves on ever constantly striving
Addicted to seeking and afraid of arriving.
You're traveling fast at the speed of surviving
With fear in the driver's seat doing the driving.

No trust is a must, you must always be worried.
No peace till deceased, you must always be hurried.
The joys of each moment go swishing on by
As the ego keeps reaching for pies in the sky.

Groping and grasping with arms that are flailing
The ego loves giving you an F for your failings!

Or perhaps you are on the fast track of success.
You're constantly driven to be great, better, best!

You're a mover, a shaker, a big-time achiever.
You're a real self-made man, a dazzling diva.
You're rich and you're famous and make quite a splash.
You're on top of the world and you're rolling in cash.

You drive the right car; you've married the right spouse.
Today lunch with Oprah, tomorrow the White House.
 But at night insecurity pays you a call
'Cause you know anytime that you could lose it all.

Your shrink says to rest and your spouse sure agrees.
Your doctor says, "Ulcers, take fourteen of these."
You know you should slow it down sooner or later,
 But your foot is just glued to the accelerator.

Your ego consoles, *Well, at least we're successful.*
It's a sign of success to be constantly stressful.
You've made it to prime time and everyone loves you,
But your self-esteem's based on what others think of you.
And opinions can change in the blink of an eye
Which is why you need meds just to sleep and get by.

One day when you've failed and succeeded enough,
You witness your ego exposed in the buff,
And you realize without all its protective clothing
That the ego is hiding a state of self-loathing.

And beyond that you find out the biggest of deals
You've dreamt up the ego, it's not even real!
So for richer, for poorer, in all kinds of health,
You commit to the journey of loving yourself.

You release the projections you placed upon others
And find through forgiveness that peace is discovered.
You realize the love that you searched for outside you
Is what you are made of and can't be denied you.

So you let go your worries, your plans, and your pills.
Put some logs on the fire and learn how to chill.
Your old superstitions have gone up in smoke.
(Like you can't rest in peace till after you croak.)
You no longer fear death or for that matter life
'Cause you know that all matters are gift wrapped in light.

While resting in peace you will soon be inspired
To go out in the world with some newfound desires.
Desires that spring from your heart and your soul
And wherever they take you, you're going there wholo,

'Cause your ego is now in the passenger seat.
It rolls down the window and takes in the treats.
You're not in a hurry; you're taking it slow,
'Cause the journey's as rich as the places you'll go.
Where you are going you don't need to know
For the journey's as rich as the places you'll go.

Donald's Song

New Lyrics by Scott Grace

Sung to the Tune of *Danny's Song,* by **Loggins and Messina,** *(Even though we don't have money, I'm so in love with you honey, etc.),* but as if Donald Trump had written the words about himself, honestly and vulnerably:

People say I'm insecure underneath it all,

That I build my towers tall

To compensate for something small.

Had me three trophy wives with looks that kill,

But in bed two went chill.

Glad I had pre-nuptials.

And even though I can't keep a honey,

I'm so in love with my money.

Every day I make a million more,

And in the morning when I rise

I pull the wig right over my eyes

And tell myself all day… that I'm always right.

Ran for President 'cause it was mega-fun
And I loved the attention.
Holy shit! I really won!

And even though I miss Trump Tower
I'm so in love with my power.
Look at me! I'm king of the world!

And at night when I can't sleep,
I take my phone to the can and I tweet
Anything that comes to my amazing mind.

This Earth Is Our Earth

New words by Scott Grace

Everybody breathes oxygen. Everybody is a citizen.
Everyone a potential friend, on this our earth.
Everybody breathes oxygen. Everybody is a citizen.
Everyone a potential friend, on this our earth

This earth is your earth; this earth is our earth,
from the Americas, to the streets of Asia.
From the mighty mountains, to majestic oceans,
this earth is here for you and me.

If you saw our home from outer space, you would
not see countries, you would not see race.
You'd just see beauty, a blue and white planet,
spinning and providing gravity.

This earth is your earth; this earth is our earth,
from the people of Africa, to the folks in Europe.
From the Israelis, to the Palestinians, this earth
supports everybody.

And as we're learning, ever so gradually, to get
along with folks, who have their differences.
So many languages, six thousand, nine hundred
and nine, this earth supports diversity.

Everybody breathes oxygen. Everybody is a citizen.
Everyone a potential friend, on this our earth.
Everybody breathes oxygen. Everybody is a citizen.
Everyone a potential friend, on this our earth.

Trees are so beautiful; they are our best friends.
They take our CO_2, and give us oxygen.
And as we learn to care for our beloved home,
sweet home, she can take care of you and me.

Time to say bye-bye to fossil fuels and build a new
economy on alternative energy.
Like wind and solar, electric cars and planes.
Urgency, emergency, brings out the best in
humanity.

This earth is your earth; this earth is our earth, from
those with private jets to those in poverty.
Every hungry child is our responsibility; this earth
can feed everybody. This earth supports
everybody; this earth is here for you and me.

Everybody breathes oxygen. Everybody is a citizen.
Everyone a potential friend, on this our earth.
Everybody breathes oxygen. Everybody is a citizen.
Everyone is an immigrant, on this our earth.

Everybody breathes oxygen. Everybody is a citizen.
Everyone a potential friend, on this our earth.
Everybody breathes oxygen. Everybody is a citizen.
Everyone a potential friend, on this our earth.

ABOUT THE AUTHOR

Scott Grace sings and speaks and leads workshops on healing and awakening. He has a book on Amazon called *Teach Me How to Love: A True Story that Opens Hearts and Helps with the Laundry*.

He is perhaps best known for crafting Song Portraits.

A Song Portrait is a personal, custom-made song, performed with voice and guitar that honors and celebrates your loved one, alive or deceased.

A Song Portrait can also be created for yourself, your business, your website, or for a cause you believe in.

A Song Portrait is a gift that will be listened to over and over again, and treasured for a lifetime. You can hear samples at

www.scottsongs.com/song-portraits/

In addition he has been a stand-up comic that has opened up for Robin Williams and Dana Carvey, made nine CD's of his music, and loves to present at conferences, corporate events, and just about anywhere he is invited.

A master at improvisational on-the-spot song writing, he is also known as the *Spiritual Dr. Seuss*, and has received close to three million hits from just four of his numerous poems on YouTube.

Find out more at:
www.scottsongs.com

Scott is also an intuitive coach and guide. If you are sensing you can use some help surfing the intense changes of these times, political and personal, if you want support in finding your higher ground while the earth shakes, shoot Scott an email.

scott@scottsongs.com

Or you can read about his coaching practice at:
www.scottsongs.com/life-coaching/

www.ingramcontent.com/pod-product-compliance
Lightning Source LLC
Chambersburg PA
CBHW071307040426
42444CB00009B/1911